The Demography of Forced Migration

Summary of a Workshop

GW00320145

Holly Reed, John Haaga, and Charles Keely, editors

Committee on Population
Commission on Behavioral and Social Sciences and Education
National Research Council

NATIONAL ACADEMY PRESS
Washington, DC   1998

NATIONAL ACADEMY PRESS • 2101 Constitution Ave., NW • Washington, DC 20418

NOTICE: The project that is the subject of this report was approved by the Governing Board of the National Research Council (NRC), whose members are drawn from the councils of the National Academy of Sciences, the National Academy of Engineering, and the Institute of Medicine. The members of the committee responsible for the report were chosen for their special competences and with regard for appropriate balance.

The National Academy of Sciences is a private, nonprofit, self-perpetuating society of distinguished scholars engaged in scientific and engineering research, dedicated to the furtherance of science and technology and to their use for the general welfare. Upon the authority of the charter granted to it by the Congress in 1863, the Academy has a mandate that requires it to advise the federal government on scientific and technical matters. Dr. Bruce M. Alberts is president of the National Academy of Sciences.

The National Academy of Engineering was established in 1964, under the charter of the National Academy of Sciences, as a parallel organization of outstanding engineers. It is autonomous in its administration and in the selection of its members, sharing with the National Academy of Sciences the responsibility for advising the federal government. The National Academy of Engineering also sponsors engineering programs aimed at meeting national needs, encourages education and research, and recognizes the superior achievements of engineers. Dr. William A. Wulf is president of the National Academy of Engineering.

The Institute of Medicine was established in 1970 by the National Academy of Sciences to secure the services of eminent members of appropriate professions in the examination of policy matters pertaining to the health of the public. The Institute acts under the responsibility given to the National Academy of Sciences by its congressional charter to be an adviser to the federal government and, upon its own initiative, to identify issues of medical care, research, and education. Dr. Kenneth I. Shine is president of the Institute of Medicine.

The National Research Council was organized by the National Academy of Sciences in 1916 to associate the broad community of science and technology with the Academy's purposes of furthering knowledge and advising the federal government. Functioning in accordance with general policies determined by the Academy, the Council has become the principal operating agency of both the National Academy of Sciences and the National Academy of Engineering in providing services to the government, the public, and the scientific and engineering communities. The Council is administered jointly by both Academies and the Institute of Medicine. Dr. Bruce M. Alberts is chairman of the National Research Council.

This project was funded by a grant from the Andrew W. Mellon Foundation. Any opinions, findings, conclusions, or recommendations expressed in this publication are those of the authors and do not necessarily reflect the view of the organization that provided support for the project.

International Standard Book Number 0-309-06141-5

Additional copies of this report are available from:
National Academy Press
2101 Constitution Avenue, NW
Washington, DC 20418
Call 800-624-6242 or 202-334-3313 (in the Washington Metropolitan Area).
This report is also available on line at http://www.nap.edu

PARTICIPANTS
WORKSHOP ON THE DEMOGRAPHY OF FORCED MIGRATION

Presenters

THOMAS ARGENT, U.S. Committee for Refugees, Washington, D.C.

JON BENNETT, The Global IDP Survey, Oxford, England

RICHARD BLACK, School of African and Asian Studies, University of Sussex

BRENT BURKHOLDER, International Emergency and Refugee Health Program, Centers for Disease Control and Prevention, U.S. Department of Health and Human Services

GREGORY GARBINSKY, Office of Foreign Disaster Assistance, U.S. Agency for International Development

STEVEN HANSCH, Refugee Policy Group, Washington, D.C.

ALLAN G. HILL, Center for Population and Development Studies, Harvard University

KENNETH HILL, Department of Population Dynamics, Johns Hopkins University

BELA HOVY, Program Coordination Section, United Nations High Commissioner for Refugees, Geneva, Switzerland

CHARLES KEELY, Department of Demography, Georgetown University

W. COURTLAND ROBINSON, School of Public Health, Johns Hopkins University

THE HONORABLE THOMAS C. SAWYER, U.S. House of Representatives

SUSANNE SCHMEIDL, Consultant, Program Coordination Section, United Nations High Commissioner for Refugees, Geneva, Switzerland

RONALD WALDMAN, BASICS, Arlington, Virginia

MYRON WEINER, Department of Political Science, Massachusetts Institute of Technology

Other Participants

JENNIFER ADAMS, Center for Population, Health, and Nutrition, U.S. Agency for International Development

NAOMI BLUMBERG, Center for Population, Health, and Nutrition, U.S. Agency for International Development

GILBERT BURNHAM, School of Public Health, Johns Hopkins University

BARNEY COHEN, Committee on Population, National Research Council

PETER J. DONALDSON, Population Reference Bureau, Washington, D.C.

LINDA GORDON, Office of Policy and Planning, U.S. Immigration and Naturalization Service

JOHN HAAGA, Committee on Population, National Research Council

DAVID HAINES, Department of Sociology and Anthropology, George Mason University
KIMBERLY HAMILTON, The Howard W. Gilman Foundation, New York
NANCY PENDARVIS HARRIS, John Snow, Inc., Arlington, Virginia
STEVEN HAWKINS, Center for Population, Health, and Nutrition, U.S. Agency for International Development
MIN LIU, Population Reference Bureau, Washington, D.C.
CAROLYN MAKINSON, The Andrew W. Mellon Foundation, New York
JAMES McCARTHY, Center for Population and Family Health, Columbia University
FAITH MITCHELL, Division on Social and Economic Studies, National Research Council
BARBARA MONAHAN, CARE International, Atlanta
PAULA NERSESIAN, BASICS, Arlington, Virginia
KATHLEEN NEWLAND, Carnegie Endowment for International Peace, Washington, D.C.
SHIRLIE PINKHAM, Bureau of Population, Refugees, and Migration, U.S. Department of State
HOLLY REED, Committee on Population, National Research Council
PAUL SPIEGEL, School of Public Health, Johns Hopkins University
ELLEN STARBIRD, Center for Population, Health, and Nutrition, U.S. Agency for International Development
JEREMIAH SULLIVAN, Demographic and Health Surveys, Macro International, Calverton, Maryland
SUSAN TOOLE, Women's Commission for Refugee Women and Children, New York
BARBARA BOYLE TORREY, Commission on Behavioral and Social Sciences and Education, National Research Council
SAMANTHA WHEELER, The Andrew W. Mellon Foundation, New York
MICHAEL WHITE, Department of Sociology, Brown University
BRADLEY WOODRUFF, International Emergency and Refugee Health Program, Centers for Disease Control and Prevention, U.S. Department of Health and Human Services
HANIA ZLOTNIK, Population Division, United Nations, New York

Acknowledgments

This report summarizes presentations and discussions at the Workshop on the Demography of Forced Migration, organized by the Committee on Population of the National Research Council (NRC), in Washington, DC, November 6-7, 1997. The workshop was funded by the Andrew W. Mellon Foundation.

The workshop would not have been possible without the efforts of several people, but two deserve special recognition. The committee was extremely fortunate in being able to enlist the services of Professor Charles Keely of Georgetown University, a member emeritus of the Committee on Population, who collaborated on the project and helped ensure that it was a success. The committee is indebted to Carolyn Makinson of the Andrew W. Mellon Foundation for her request that led to the workshop and for her encouragement and intellectual guidance during the development of the workshop.

The committee is grateful to the staff at the National Research Council, who made it all possible. Holly Reed, research associate for the committee, provided a constant intellectual and managerial presence for the project, from the organization of the workshop to the publication of this report. Eugenia Grohman, associate director for reports for the Commission on Behavioral and Social Sciences and Education, skillfully edited the manuscript and guided it through the review process. The work was carried out under the general direction of John Haaga and Barney Cohen, the former and current directors of the committee, respectively.

The report has been reviewed by individuals chosen for their diverse perspectives and technical expertise, in accordance with procedures approved by the Report Review Committee of the NRC. The purpose of this independent review is to provide candid and critical comments that will assist the authors and the

NRC in making the published report as sound as possible and to ensure that the report meets institutional standards for objectivity, evidence, and responsiveness to the purpose of the activity. The content of the review comments and the draft manuscript remain confidential to protect the integrity of the deliberative process.

We thank the following individuals for their participation in the review of this report: Caroline H. Bledsoe, Department of Anthropology, Northwestern University; W. Henry Mosley, School of Public Health, Johns Hopkins University; Alberto Palloni, Department of Sociology, University of Wisconsin; and T. Paul Schultz, Department of Economics, Yale University. While these individuals provided constructive comments and suggestions, responsibility for the final content of this report rests solely with the authoring committee and the NRC.

Most of all, of course, we are grateful to all the dedicated participants in the workshop, whose ideas and comments are summarized here; we hope that this publication helps ensure that their work will continue to contribute to the growing international field of forced migration studies.

Jane Menken, Chair
Committee on Population

Contents

The Demography of Forced Migration: Summary of a Workshop

INTRODUCTION

There may be as many as 50 million forced migrants in the world today, and that number is growing. A forced migrant can be defined roughly as someone who is forced to leave his or her home because of a real or perceived threat to life or well-being. Often many people in the same area leave their homes at once due to war or violence, leading to massive movements of forced migrants. When such people move within their own country, they are known as internally displaced persons; if they cross a border into another country, they are usually considered refugees.[1] Because forced migration situations are often physically dangerous and politically complicated, estimates of these populations are often difficult to make. Estimates of forced migration vary, but it is probable that there are about 23 million refugees and more than 30 million internally displaced people. The number of refugees has fallen somewhat in the past few years, while the number of internally displaced persons has been rising rapidly.

In order to assist specific groups of forced migrants and also to better understand the general plight of forced migrants, good demographic data are needed. However, collecting data on forced migration presents tremendous challenges for normal data collection processes and standards.

Under normal conditions, the collection of demographic data, although not entirely problem free, is a fairly straightforward process. Demographic data are most often collected about populations with a permanent residence. Data are

---

[1]These are general definitions of these terms. Defining forced migrants is a much-debated topic; see below, "Defining the Status of Forced Migrants," for further discussion.

1

usually collected by government agencies, private organizations, and researchers who intend to use the data for purposes that range from making policy to marketing to scholarly inquiry. Although data may be time sensitive, the conditions under which they are collected are usually safe. Those who collect data are trained professionals who use methods that are generally established and orderly. Often data on many different aspects of people's lives are collected at the same time to facilitate subsequent analysis.

These standard processes for collecting demographic data are severely challenged in the situation of forced migration. Frequently, forced migration involves a life-threatening situation in which survival is key, and data collection is certainly not a primary concern. Even when data are collected in such situations, the conditions do not permit standard data collection processes. Rapidly shifting populations, physical danger, and chaotic circumstances create difficulties for data collectors and affect the precision of data, and the people who are collecting the data may not be adequately trained and supervised. In addition, various political motivations can compromise the data collection and accuracy of the data. These factors make it clear that precise data on forced migrants may be impossible to obtain.

For some purposes, such as emergency relief, precise data may not be critical. Relief workers usually need data immediately in order to estimate needs for emergency rations, shelter, and medical supplies, and approximate numbers are more than adequate for this purpose. Approximate numbers may also be sufficient to raise concern for a particular crisis and mobilize political attention.

Although agencies providing emergency relief have one set of needs—rough counts of populations for whom they will be responsible—other organizations have different needs that may not be satisfied by imprecise estimates. Forced migrant situations can last for years or even decades, and international agencies, governments of countries of asylum, and governments of countries of resettlement may all be involved in planning for the migrants. Forced migrants who are not in camps, under formal protection, or receiving relief services may be the hardest to count, but they also may most need the attention of the international community.

Furthermore, without minimizing the primary need for numbers to plan service delivery and to inform policy debates, it is also important to keep in mind the need for historical understanding. The situations that create forced migration are tragic. Social science can contribute to understanding the dynamics and causes of a given situation, but that work requires accurate demographic data. There are many examples for which careful demographic analysis after the fact has increased understanding of important events of the twentieth century, including the Armenian diaspora, the "great leap forward" in China, the Sahelian famines, and the Indochina Wars. Although such studies may be too late to be of immediate use in those particular situations, they may help to understand how to deal with similar situations in the future.

To explore a range of issues about internally displaced persons and refugees, the Committee on Population of the National Research Council organized a Workshop on the Demography of Forced Migration in Washington, D.C., in November 1997. The purpose of the workshop was to investigate the ways in which population and other social scientists can produce more useful demographic information about forced migrant populations and how they differ.

This report summarizes the background papers prepared for the meeting, the presentations, and the general discussion. The summary follows the basic order of the meeting: general population estimates were discussed in the first session, population compositions and vital rates followed in a second session, and the final session focused on a possible future research agenda. This summary is necessarily brief, and interested readers are referred to the cited works or to the participants for more information. The meeting was intended to elicit a wide range of views and provoke discussion about a major issue in the world today.

POPULATION ESTIMATES

Defining the Status of Forced Migrants

The topic of definitions and nomenclature generated a great deal of discussion during the workshop. Populations that have been displaced for reasons other than environmental disaster or economic crisis can all be considered forced migrants. These include many groups, some of whom are very difficult to identify and some of whom are already identified as populations of concern. Steven Hansch created the continuum shown in Figure 1 to illustrate some different types of populations under the umbrella term of "forced migrants." The large number of groups, many of which have ambiguous status, creates confusion about who is in which category. Hansch discussed the fact that definitions are fairly well accepted for groups on the righthand side of the continuum, for which people have a specific legal status and are contained in a small area, such as refugees living in camps. Yet when the universe is unknown and people are spread over a large area, the definitions and legal status become more indefinite, and the ability to count these groups becomes complicated.

Even when one looks more closely at specific groups, the definitions are not always clearer. The most basic definition of a "refugee" in international law is the definition adopted by the United Nations in the 1951 Convention Relating to the Status of Refugees and extended in the subsequent 1967 Protocol (United Nations, 1950:Article 1, Section A(2); United Nations, 1966: Article 1):[2]

---

[2]The 1951 Convention definition was restricted to refugees in Europe following the end of World War II. The 1967 Protocol removed the geographical and chronological limitations to make the definition more general. However, some nations that are party to the Convention have not signed the Protocol, and vice versa.

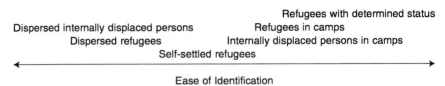

Refugees with determined status
Dispersed internally displaced persons   Refugees in camps
Dispersed refugees   Internally displaced persons in camps
Self-settled refugees

←——→

Ease of Identification

Most difficult to identify: Easiest to identify:
universe unknown;   universe known; defined
wide geographical spread   geographical spread

FIGURE 1   Forced migrant populations of concern. SOURCE: Adapted from Steven
Hansch, Refugee Policy Group, Washington, D.C.

> Any person who owing to a well-founded fear of being persecuted for reasons
> of race, religion, nationality, membership of a particular social group or politi-
> cal opinion, is outside the country of his nationality and is unable, or owing to
> such fear, is unwilling to avail himself of the protection of that country; or who,
> not having a nationality and being outside the country of his former habitual
> residence as a result of such events, is unable or, owing to such fear, is unwill-
> ing to return to it.

Refugees who fall under this definition are often known as "Convention"
refugees. In contrast, "mandate" or "statutory" refugees fall under the mandate
of the United Nations High Commissioner for Refugees (UNHCR), as declared
in its 1950 statute,[3] and are only two of the groups of persons of concern to
UNHCR. Statistics on forced migrants who come under the mandate of the
United Nations Relief and Works Agency for Palestine Refugees in the Near East
are not included in UNHCR's estimates (U.N. High Commissioner for Refugees,
1997). Hence, even UNHCR, a primary source for most statistics on forced
migrants, uses different definitions to serve different groups, and by extension, to
collect data on these groups (U.N. High Commissioner for Refugees, 1997:1):

> Refugees, which includes:
>
> a) persons recognized as refugees by Governments having ratified the 1951
> Convention and/or 1967 Protocol;

---

[3]The definition of "refugee" found in the UNHCR Statute is very similar to that found in the
Convention, with the addition of a clause allowing for those who were previously considered refugees according to international law (under the Arrangements of 1926 or 1928, the Conventions of
1933 or 1938, the Protocol of 1939, or the Constitution of the International Refugee Organization) to
be considered refugees for the UNHCR's purposes.

b) persons recognized as refugees under the 1969 OAU Convention and the principles of the Cartagena Declaration;

c) persons recognized by UNHCR as refugees in accordance with its Statute ("mandate" refugees);

d) persons who have been granted temporary protection on a group basis.

Returnees: persons who were of concern to UNHCR when they were outside their country of origin and who remain so for a limited time after their return.

Others: asylum-seekers, others in a refugee-like situation who have not been granted refugee status ("humanitarian" refugees).

Internally displaced: persons displaced internally within their country for reasons that would make them of concern to UNHCR if they were outside of their country of origin.

Still another definition comes from the U.S. Committee for Refugees (USCR) (1997:4), which reports:

two categories of people in need of protection and/or assistance: refugees, who are unwilling or unable to return to their home countries because they fear persecution or violence there; and asylum-seekers, who claim that they are refugees.

USCR statistics also generally do not include persons who have been granted permanent status (U.S. Committee for Refugees, 1997).

From these definitions it may seem that the key difference is whether the people counted have permanent or temporary status, but there are other sources of definitional variance. In order to account for all persons who may be in need of protection and assistance, including those who may not be "official" refugees, USCR keeps statistics on a category of "selected populations in refugee-like situations." These displaced populations are people whose legal status is unclear, such as Palestinians in Jordan who were displaced from the West Bank in 1967, the Burmese in Thailand who may be refugees but might also be economic migrants, and "forced migrants" from the former Soviet republics (Argent, 1997). It is possible that, due to the more liberal definitions used, some of USCR's data contain a number of economic migrants.

Of course, since most UNHCR and USCR statistics come from governments themselves, a key to understanding the data is knowing how various governments define and count forced migrants. Generally, it seems that industrialized countries tend to use the Convention definition, since they usually grant refugee status on an individual basis (Schmeidl, 1995). However, the definitions of refugee found in the 1969 Organization of African Unity (OAU) Convention and the 1984 Cartagena Declaration make it evident that such a narrow interpretation does not always work for developing regions: they often use a definition that allows for recognition of the group displacement caused by systemic violence and internal conflict. It is not the status of individuals that matters in such situations, but rather the well-being and protection of the group.

Yet not all developing nations have adopted the OAU Convention or the Cartagena Declaration definitions. Many other nations have not signed either the U.N. Convention or Protocol or both. The guidelines and process used to determine if a person fits the specific interpretation of the accepted definition of refugee in a particular country may vary widely. Therefore, the numbers of refugees estimated by governments (and in turn, many of the estimates produced by UNHCR and USCR) are, at best, a representation of a government's criteria and procedures for refugees (Bilsborrow et al., 1997).

An international organization may disagree with a government's interpretation of the situation and cite persons as refugees even when their state of asylum might not view them as such. For example, USCR cites approximately 30,000 refugees from Mali and Niger living in Algeria. These persons are ethnic Tuaregs, known to be a nomadic population; the Algerian government does not recognize them as refugees and classifies them as economic migrants. This difference (along with the Tuaregs' life-style) makes it very difficult to get an accurate estimate of how many people from Mali and Niger are actually living in Algeria, and, of those, how many are actually refugees (U.S. Commitee for Refugees, 1997).

During the discussion of definitional differences, Hania Zlotnik suggested that there were at least six different perspectives represented in the "world of forced migration." When organizations look at situations from these various viewpoints, there are likely to be several distinct definitions of who is a refugee, who is an internally displaced person, who is a repatriated refugee, and so forth. First, there is the model perspective, which is embodied in such documents as the 1951 U.N. Convention and 1967 Protocol, the OAU Convention, and the Cartagena Declaration. The definitions in these documents are usually seen as the standards by which others are measured, although, as noted, many states are not party to these definitions, and they are far from being universally accepted.

Second is the individual state perspective, which depends on whether or not a state is a party to the international instruments mentioned above, as well as the way in which that particular state determines a person's status under those definitions. A third perspective is that of humanitarian aid agencies and other nongovermental organizations: they are often most concerned with whom they assist, which may be at least partially determined by the two perspectives above, but also by the agency's individual mandate, operating procedures, and funds.

The fourth perspective is the advocacy group point of view: protection of those who have been forced to leave their homes. This perspective may result in a broader definition than the model or even the state perspective. Fifth, there are scholars and researchers who study refugees and the problems surrounding them: researchers are often concerned about who are forced migrants, in contrast to voluntary migrants.

Finally, it is important to keep the perspective of the movers themselves in mind. They may define themselves as forced migrants because they feel they were "forced" to move, but the international community may not define them as refugees or internally displaced persons. As Zlotnik pointed out, all of these competing points of view make it nearly impossible to come to a consensus on a single definition of who is a forced migrant.

Estimating Forced Migrant Populations

The two major agencies that publish statistics on refugees and forced migrant populations are the UNHCR and USCR. Bela Hovy of UNHCR explained that its statistics are mostly obtained from national governments' own records and estimates that are collected through its annual statistical survey (see, e.g., U.N. High Commissioner for Refugees, 1997). The agency sometimes relies on other sources as well, such as local governments, opposition groups, religious authorities, local and international relief agencies, other U.N. agencies, or foreign military authorities. If reliable numbers are not available from any of these sources, registration in camps is often used. Yet registration of forced migrants may not be suitable if the situation seems to be very temporary (tribal conflicts or natural disasters) or if the migrants have "self-settled," that is, intermingled with local people, often of the same clan or ethnicity, who may be assisting them (U.N. High Commissioner for Refugees, 1994). In addition, Hovy noted that registration statistics are usually beneficiary numbers that are used to keep track of how many people a program is serving. Therefore, they are likely to be inaccurate counts of everyone who is displaced. For this reason, UNHCR does not use registration numbers as the only, nor even the major, source of its data.

During the very early stages of a crisis, rapid assessments are undertaken, often by a Disaster Assistance Response Team (DART) dispatched by the Bureau for Humanitarian Response of the Office of Foreign Disaster Assistance of the U.S. Agency for International Development, usually on the request of UNHCR. Gregory Garbinsky explained that DARTs were originally created to respond to natural disasters but that their purpose has been expanded due to the increased number of complex humanitarian emergencies involving refugees and internally displaced persons in recent years. These teams use various techniques from aerial photography to simple visual assessments in order to estimate rapidly the numbers of those in need during the onset of a crisis. Since the goal of a DART is to meet the immediate, critical needs of those affected by the disaster, the team does not remain after the emergency phase has ended.

After the crisis phase is over, if registration is not feasible, household or family surveys are sometimes used. All of these various techniques and sources are reflected in the numbers reported by UNHCR in its annual *Statistical Overview*. In the explanatory notes accompanying these statistics, there is usually specific information on the origins of particular population estimates for each host country. Nevertheless, it is not always clear which methods or sources UNHCR used to produce a given estimate.

Thomas Argent of the USCR explained that it produces its own estimates, which are based on many different sources. If several different estimates of a displaced population are available, then USCR examines each estimate for likely biases and makes an independent assessment based on the judgment of its staff. Some estimates may come primarily from site visits conducted by USCR staff; these often differ from other estimates, such as UNHCR's.

In addition, Argent explained that USCR is especially wary of reported numbers of internally displaced persons; these populations are often extremely difficult to count due to their isolation and lack of official status. For these populations, the organization often relies on its own site visits for more accurate figures (Argent, 1997). The rationale behind USCR's choice of numbers is usually explained in the country reports found in the *World Refugee Survey*. For example, although the government of Uzbekistan claimed that some 40,000 refugees and other asylum seekers from other countries were living there by December 1996, UNHCR had registered only around 3,000 official asylum seekers. In this instance, USCR reported the lower number (U.S. Committee for Refugees, 1997).

Differences Between Data Sources

Susanne Schmeidl reviewed several reasons that data on forced migrants may differ between the two major sources (UNHCR and USCR) and why the data in general may be unreliable. First, the people are on the move, which makes enumeration difficult in unstable situations. For example, there is a group of Afghans who continually migrate across the border between Iran and Afghanistan. Their legal status as well as their total number are difficult to determine at any specific time (U.S. Committee for Refugees, 1997). Another problem is that people in the field may not be well trained in counting techniques and so reports may differ in their precision. Furthermore, the likelihood of error tends to increase when the data are transmitted through several levels before they are published.

Yet another reason for differences in numbers is that often only those who are receiving assistance from the international aid community are counted, so those who self-settle with a host population may be overlooked. For example, there is an ongoing debate between relief workers and other groups over the true number of Liberian refugees living in Guinea. Since many of them live among the local population in rural settlements, identifying these persons has been difficult for assistance and protection agencies. Many estimates of forced migrant populations may not include people who do not receive assistance.

Different recognition of the initiation of forced migrant flows can also lead to quite different estimates. If one organization does not begin counting until persons receive assistance and another counts from the start of the population flow, their numbers may vary greatly. Likewise, if one source reports those who are receiving assistance, while another simply reports those who actually entered the country during the year , the numbers will differ. For example, while UNHCR reported refugees who left Mozambique between 1969 and 1990, USCR only reported refugee flows between 1969 and 1973 and again between 1983 and 1990. It is possible that UNHCR counted all persons from Mozambique who were being assisted each year, while USCR may have only counted those who actually moved during the year (Schmeidl, 1995).

Closely related to these sorts of definitional problems are problems related to the time of reporting. In the past, USCR often reported mid-year estimates, while UNHCR generally reported end-year estimates. In the 1990s, USCR changed its reporting practice and began reporting end-year estimates as well, so comparison between the sources should no longer be affected by time reporting differences.

Rounding numbers also introduces a small amount of error to the estimates that can accumulate and lead to large overall discrepancies. All of USCR's statistics are rounded to the nearest hundred, while UNHCR often reports exact numbers.

Finally, definitions and political concerns are very important in determining who is a refugee, an asylee, an internally displaced person, or other "person of concern." Thus, numbers are likely to differ somewhat—despite the accuracy of the counting, the reporting processes, and the best intentions of field staff and others—simply because of definitional differences.

Despite all of these potential problems, however, Schmeidl (1997) found that when she compared data from both sources over a period of 20 years, the majority of the differences could be explained by variances in definitions, timing of reporting, data collection systems, and use of secondary sources. This finding underscores the critical need for organizations who report data to attempt to document sources, definitions, and data limitations as thoroughly as possible. Such information can help researchers identify potential sources of bias in the data.

Practical and Political Issues Surrounding Data Collection

It is easy to imagine the practical difficulties of counting hundred or thousands of people who are moving. If people flee a dangerous situation, the danger they are trying to escape can travel with them, or a new threat can emerge. When the slaughter of innocent refugees occurs in such places as Zaire and Bosnia, it becomes clear that in a growing number of situations, even those persons located in camps or so-called "safe areas" are not always safe from attack by bands of militias and others. Consequently, security issues are a major issue surrounding the identification of the total number of forced migrants in a crisis situation.

The sheer number of people who may be forced to migrate can make it very difficult to ensure proper enumeration, especially if the population is constantly on the move. For example, it has been estimated that during a few days in 1994, approximately 1 million Rwandans crossed the border to Zaire to escape civil war and genocide (U.S. Committee for Refugees, 1997). Even if relief agencies had foreseen this massive exodus, the logistics of counting 1 million people accurately would have required massive resources, which are simply not available in most forced migrant situations.

Moreover, forced migrant flows often occur in remote areas, away from centers of population and development. These areas may be further isolated due to a breakdown of infrastructure caused by the political crisis (Levine et al., 1985). For instance, relief workers trying to assist Sudanese refugees in Uganda in 1996 were often unable to reach the refugees because of land mines and road closings (U.S. Committee for Refugees, 1997). Under such circumstances, it may be difficult to reach the migrants, either to count them or to assist them.

The phenomenon of self-settlement can also create problems for those trying to estimate forced migrant populations. Refugees may not dwell in camps, but instead settle with the local population, who may share a similar language, ethnicity, or even kinship ties. For example, many of the Togolese refugees in Benin are self-settled refugees (U.S. Committee for Refugees, 1997). Self-settlement can make it very difficult for assistance groups to determine who actually fled their homes and to get an accurate count of the forced migrants without accidentally including some of the local population (U.N. High Commissioner for Refugees, 1994).

Even when refugees do reside in camps, there are numerous ways for errors to occur in the counts. For example, refugees might misinform relief workers about their own numbers. They might be inclined to report larger numbers of refugees than there are in order to get larger food rations, or they may subvert attempts to get an accurate count because of fear (U.N. High Commissioner for Refugees, 1994). Relief workers might also be guilty of overreporting of the numbers of forced migrants in an attempt to encourage more aid. For example, a recent report revealed that estimates of the number of internally displaced persons in one African country had been exaggerated by 60 percent in an apparent attempt to leverage more relief supplies (Argent, 1997). In other situations, aid workers may underestimate the number of actual migrants by accident. In addition, refugees might leave a camp to return home without notifying relief workers, or they may be hesitant to report deaths of family members because they fear that their food rations will be decreased. Whatever the reason, however, such reporting biases definitely make it more difficult to attain accurate numbers. All of these factors can contribute to a total count of persons that may be vastly different from the actual number.

Many available statistics on forced migrants are derived from registers of people who are receiving assistance from a relief program. These beneficiary statistics, often kept by governments, international organizations, or nongovermental organizations, can be very useful when no other figures are available, but their quality is also subject to debate. They may be more reliable if persons are in closed camps, where their movements are restricted (Bilsborrow et al., 1997), but keeping refugees in such camps may actually be detrimental to their health and well-being (Van Damme, 1995).

Forced migration is a highly charged political issue, and many people have a stake in how many refugees or internally displaced persons are counted. Government statistics may be manipulated for a variety of reasons. For example, if a regime is fighting a civil war that has displaced many persons, it might report their number as lower than it is so that the situation appears under control. Likewise, if the government is responsible for driving its own people into a neighboring country, it is likely to underreport the number of refugees.

Conversely, a state may be inclined to overstate the actual number of refugees from a bordering nation to draw negative attention to an adversary or in an attempt to gain more relief aid for the refugees. Sometimes governments will refuse to allow international organizations access to the refugee populations within their borders, which makes it nearly impossible to disprove their suspicious statistics (U.N. High Commissioner for Refugees, 1994). In an unstable situation, when the truth is being exaggerated or twisted by several different sources, it can become nearly impossible to arrive at an accurate figure.

In a presentation of the political and practical issues surrounding the collection of forced migrant statistics, Richard Black raised two primary points. First, accountability to donors can cloud the collection of data. For example, it can lead to false precision as assistance agencies attempt to be responsive to donors. Black declared that agencies should be more accountable to the forced migrants themselves and less accountable to their funding sources. He reminded participants that the reason refugees and internally displaced persons are of concern to the international community is because they are in need of protection and assistance, not because they have moved from one place to another (Harrell-Bond et al., 1992).

Second, Black said that aid is too often focused on assisting solely the forced migrants themselves, rather than aiding the entire needy population in an area. As a result, keeping track of who is and who is not a refugee can become the primary task. He suggested that perhaps a movement away from targeting aid toward refugees alone and toward "universal" aid to people in need in a given area could alleviate some of the difficulties associated with counting refugees. Because aid would not be targeted so strictly, refugee numbers would not be directly linked to the quantity of aid. Then, according to Black, refugees might not be as wary of participating in their counting, especially if the enumeration is done in a humane and dignified fashion.

Although registration and censuses in refugee camps could be made simpler and more effective, Black emphasized the need to rely more on sampling techniques to obtain accurate estimates of forced migrant camps. Sampling techniques are well developed and often used in the social sciences, yet they are not commonly used in forced migrant situations. Furthermore, sample surveys can furnish relatively accurate data and are both cheaper and easier to administer than a census or registration. The failure to use sampling techniques in the field was often cited by many workshop participants as a problem with current estimation approaches.

Estimating Internally Displaced Populations

Persons who are internally displaced within their own countries are often even more difficult to count than refugees who have crossed an international border, for three reasons. First, these persons may be under attack by their own government; thus, they are often in hiding in remote locations of the countryside, which makes them inaccessible. It is also highly unlikely that a persecuting government will allow international agencies any access to these people or even that it will divulge any of its own estimates of their number. And even if such numbers were made available, they would probably be very unreliable.

A second difficulty in counting internally displaced persons is that relatively few congregate in camps or in large and distinct groupings. The forced migration situations in Burundi, Rwanda, and Afghanistan, all beginning in the early 1990s, were exceptions to this rule. The more usual phenomenon is for people to travel to urban centers and "disappear" or to stay with relatives in the vicinity of their homes (which may be just across an international border). In other cases, such as Uganda, people may hide in forests during the night and return to their homes during the day. Such situations lead to the question: how long one can be classified as an internally displaced person, rather than someone who has made a permanent move to a different home? In Lebanon, for example, most of the internally displaced have been away from their original homes for 25 years without a "durable" solution.

A third reason that internally displaced persons are difficult to count is that they have not crossed an international border and their status under international law is ambiguous. Usually, they have few or no legal rights and protections. Although in recent years UNHCR has been asked by the Secretary General and by the Security Council of the United Nations to consider certain groups of internally displaced persons as "populations of concern," this does not mean that they are all counted or that it is always clear who they are. USCR estimated the number of internally displaced persons worldwide in 1996 to be more than 19 million, but it admits that the number may be much higher because assessments may be "fragmentary and unreliable" (U.S. Committee for Refugees, 1997:6).

Although the number of refugees worldwide has been decreasing steadily in recent years, the number of internally displaced people has been growing rapidly, due mostly to the ever-shifting international norms regarding refugee policy. Containing conflicts in their place of origin has taken precedence over the offering of sanctuary in other countries. Therefore, many people are displaced within their own countries, where their lives may be in danger and where they are usually unable to receive assistance from the international community (Bennett, 1997).

Jon Bennett discussed the working definition of internally displaced person that was recently adopted by the United Nations (Bennett, 1997:1): [4]

> Persons (or groups of persons) who have been forced to flee or to leave their homes or places of habitual residence as a result of, or in order to avoid, in particular, the effects of armed conflict, situations of generalized violence, violations of human rights or natural or human-made disasters, and who have not crossed an internationally recognized state border.

As Bennett pointed out, many criticize the definition, and no one is satisfied with the term "internally displaced person." In a crisis situation, a person's official legal status can change rapidly, depending on the nature of the immediate threat, where the person is located, and other factors. Yet the needs of such displaced persons remain the same, in spite of their quickly changing legal status. Although the emphasis is on people who have been forced to flee violence or human rights violations, victims of natural disaster are included as internally displaced persons under the current working definition. This inclusion is intended to give the international aid community more leeway to assist such people, but it can create confusion when interpreting trends in internally displaced persons over time.

Bennett stated his view that USCR is currently the best source of data on internally displaced persons, although UNHCR has also published some estimates in recent years. Results from the Global Internally Displaced Person Survey, to be published in 1998, will combine data and knowledge of internally displaced persons in one volume, which will increase the amount of information available.

Internally displaced persons are also difficult to count because it is sometimes hard to distinguish between voluntary migrants and true internally displaced persons. Finally, it is difficult to determine when a person is no longer internally displaced, or when he or she has been "reintegrated" into their community. This problem is similar to that facing those who count repatriated refugees. In other words, although people may have returned to their homeland, that does not necessarily mean that they have returned *home*.

Charles Keely reminded the participants that a refugee situation is very different politically from a situation of internal displacement. Because refugee

---

[4]This definition has been adapted over time by the U.N.'s Special Representative on Internally Displaced Persons and used by the Global Internally Displaced Person Survey. The UNHCR definition is slightly more restrictive, with an emphasis only on those who would be "Convention" refugees had they crossed a border.

flows indicate that the state system is not working properly, other states will usually intervene to fix the problem. If people are displaced within their own country, however, other states may not even know about the problem. If they do, they have little incentive (and even strong disincentive) to interfere. Thus, as Keely emphasized, estimates of internally displaced persons are ultimately biased by the interests of the states involved.

POPULATION COMPOSITION AND VITAL RATES

Estimating components of population change, such as fertility and mortality, can be much more difficult to account for in an emergency situation than under normal circumstances. Information such as the number of births or deaths, ages, and family relationships may be difficult to obtain from forced migrants themselves. And even if the refugees or internally displaced persons are willing to give information about demographic events or characteristics, relief workers may record these data in ways that do not correspond to Western statistical standards. These factors can often make it difficult to ascertain the true meaning of the statistics and further confuse the process of collecting information (U.N. High Commissioner for Refugees, 1994).

Estimating Population Composition

Estimates of population age and sex composition are needed both for planning services and for estimating and comparing mortality and fertility rates. High-risk groups that require special public health interventions, such as special feeding programs or immunizations, are most likely to be children under 5 years of age, pregnant women, and the elderly. Yet several participants noted the lack of information on population compositions in the literature on forced migration.

Various standard demographic breakdowns of populations have been created by different organizations. One nongovernmental organization uses at least three separate references to estimate the size of the various groups within a refugee population (Sandra Krause, American Refugee Committee, personal communication, 7/24/97). If the total size of the population is known (or estimated fairly well), one can then determine the numbers of vulnerable groups by using standard percentages.

A commonly quoted figure is that about 80 percent of most refugee populations are comprised of women and children under the age of 18. Although this proportion may seem high to the casual observer, it is really not very surprising. Emphasizing the proportion of women and children in the population may be important from a policy and relief standpoint, but, demographically, a refugee population might look very similar to any population in the developing world.

Estimating Mortality Rates

The first reason that mortality estimates are difficult to obtain in many forced migrant situations is because there is usually no existing vital registration system. If a registration system is in place, it is likely to break down in an emergency. Yet even if complete registration data were available, they would be likely to be flawed. Deaths are often underreported because people may fear that their family food rations will be reduced if their family size decreases. Cultural taboos about death may also lead to underreporting. Because the total population, which is the denominator when calculating mortality rates, is commonly overestimated, mortality rates are much more likely to be understated than overstated (Toole and Waldman, 1997). In addition, in order to estimate age-sex-specific mortality rates, one needs to know the composition of the population, and this information, if available, is often faulty.

Estimates are thought to be most reliable in situations in which refugees are in an organized camp setting and least reliable where internally displaced persons are spread over a large area. Generalizing findings beyond a specific sample is difficult, however, because of differing survey methods and lack of data on groups that are hard to locate or count.

Brent Burkholder discussed methods for estimating mortality rates in refugee camps. Because the total number of persons is used as the denominator when calculating a crude mortality rate, estimating the size of the entire population is important. Burkholder used the example of Goma, Zaire, in the summer of 1994 to illustrate how different methods of counting the total population led to very different estimates. Médecins Sans Frontières marked grids on crude maps to show population densities of certain areas. Individuals within selected areas were enumerated and their numbers extrapolated to provide an estimate of the total number of persons in the camps, which was 750,000. The French military, on the other hand, counted the number of shelters in aerial photographs and extrapolated from small ground surveys of population density to estimate a total number of 500,000; this count was likely to be an underestimate because many people did not have shelters at that point.

The second important component of an estimated crude mortality rate is the total number of deaths over a period of time. Burkholder discussed several collection techniques for mortality data in emergency situations. Techniques range from burial site observation to collection of hospital or death records to surveys of community leaders or the population as a whole. In Goma, it was difficult to hide deaths (which refugees might have been inclined to do to avoid losing food rations) because graves could not be dug in the volcanic soil. Body collectors were employed to count the number of dead. At first, this led to overestimates of mortality because many collectors believed that they would be paid per body. As Burkholder explained, after this misunderstanding was cleared up, the estimates were thought to be fairly reliable.

Ronald Waldman laid out a model of how the mortality rate typically changes over time in an emergency situation; see Figure 2. During the beginning of a crisis (Phase 1), mortality may rise slightly. Once the distress is great, the mortality rate usually jumps, as seen in Phase 2 of the figure. When humanitarian assistance teams begin to arrive (Phase 3), the mortality rate usually declines rapidly. Finally, during Phase 4, the mortality rate stabilizes as it approaches the baseline, or normal rate, again. A classic case of this model was among Cambodian refugees in Thailand in 1979-1980. Although the crude mortality rate (CMR) was initially quite high in the Cambodian camps (around 10 deaths per 1,000 persons per month, equivalent to a crude death rate of 120/1,000 per year), it dropped rapidly as relief assistance arrived. Within 2 months the CMR had stabilized at around 1/1,000 per month, or about 12/1,000 per year (Toole et al., 1988).

Many other cases, however, do not fit the model. For example, in camps for Tigrayan refugees in Eastern Sudan (1984-1985), the initial CMR was around 25/1,000 per month or 250/1,000 per year, which is unusually high. Even after aid

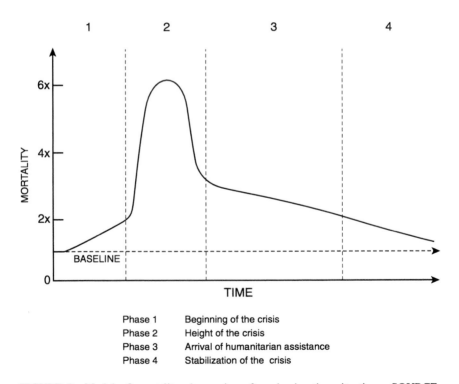

FIGURE 2 Model of mortality change in a forced migration situation. SOURCE: Ronald Waldman, BASICS, Arlington, Virginia.

arrived, the CMR remained high for over 6 months and did not stabilize until approximately 8 months after the crisis began (Toole et al., 1988). Clearly, there is no single mortality pattern that applies in all forced migrant situations.

In the field, epidemiologists often rely on baseline crude mortality rate "benchmarks" to know when a situation has changed from one phase to another. As Burkholder pointed out, however, one cannot always assume that these benchmarks are accurate. He proposed that demographers help assistance teams to know how to make them more precise and also more applicable to specific situations.

The idea of estimating mortality differently during each of these different "phases" of an emergency was emphasized by Kenneth Hill. He distinguished between the acute phase and the stabilization phase. During the acute phase, approximate estimates are good enough to differentiate catastrophic mortality from more-or-less "normal" mortality. At this time, mortality rates may vary greatly from one situation to another and between groups (i.e., children may be more vulnerable than adults). It is nearly impossible to do traditional household surveys because there are no actual households and there is not enough time to process this type of data.

Once the acute phase has passed and the population begins to stabilize, it is both easier and more important to conduct sample surveys. Although people may not be living in actual households, they can be surveyed in their living arrangements. Mortality estimates during this phase should be compared with estimates for the same group made prior to the crisis or with estimates for the surrounding population (such as the host country population). Child mortality is a good general indicator of overall population health. Even 2 to 3 years after a crisis has ended, large sample surveys with detailed birth and migration histories can be very useful for learning more about mortality dynamics among forced migrants.

It is assumed that refugees are at the highest risk of mortality immediately after their arrival in a host country. They have often traveled long distances, sometimes on foot, without enough food, water, or medical care. During this first phase of a crisis, epidemiologists often find it useful to express the crude mortality rate as the number of deaths per 10,000 persons per day. Since accurate age-sex composition is usually not known, it is difficult to assess what a "normal" level of mortality is in a particular situation. Nevertheless, a situation with a CMR of greater than 1 per 10,000 per day is commonly regarded as an emergency (Toole and Waldman, 1997).

Mortality rates typically decline after the crisis phase, but the rate of decline varies greatly, usually related to how quickly and effectively international relief efforts are implemented. For example, high death rates among Cambodian refugees in Thailand in 1979 decreased to more normal levels much faster than did the death rates of Somali refugees in Ethiopia in 1988 (Centers for Disease Control and Prevention, 1992). Although the data are insufficient and often unreliable, mortality rates are probably also very high among internally displaced populations (Toole and Waldman, 1997). Allan Hill suggested that modeling mortality among forced migrant populations in various phases of an emergency could be very useful for future crisis response. This work could be done by studying data on births and deaths from past crises.

Several participants expressed the need for more sample surveys, especially during the post-crisis phase of any situation. Jeremiah Sullivan cautioned that such surveys may not be the best choice because they are retrospective and attrition and mortality are likely to be problems with any sample. Zlotnik reminded participants that even the mortality methodologies for stable populations are not fully developed, so one should not expect immediate perfection in the field of forced migration. She also stressed the need to state clearly the methods of estimation used in published articles so that others can interpret the results properly.

Estimating Fertility Rates

Very little concrete information is available or known about fertility rates in forced migrant settings. Estimated crude birth rates, based on estimates of camp size and the number of reported births, have reportedly ranged from 45 to 55 per 1,000 population. One nongovernmental organization report states: "There seems to be little doubt that women in many refugee settings are having large numbers of children" (Wulf, 1994:7).

Summarizing the scant information available on the subject, Kenneth Hill concurred that refugees are indeed bearing children and so need reproductive health care. Yet it is impossible to generalize about fertility rates in refugee settings because there appears to be enormous variation from one setting to the next. Once again, the type of data that can and should be collected depends on the maturity of the crisis. For example, during the onset of an emergency, current status measures are strongly needed. Detailed birth histories are unlikely to be useful or feasible. Instead, asking a simple question about recent pregnancies to women attending prenatal clinics may provide not only a reasonable estimate of fertility, but may also give an indication of the current health status of the population.

Kenneth Hill also emphasized the importance of using standardized measures and analyses. Most studies seem to restrict their sample to certain narrowly defined groups and disregard selectivity. For example, one study surveyed only women who already had a child under the age of 6 about their fertility. Another study looked only at marital or union fertility. Kenneth Hill stressed the need to create typologies, by comparing similarities and differences among similar populations; only then can one begin to classify situations and know how to better deal with them. Keely emphasized the need to institutionalize the available data so that it can be better used.

Hansch noted that the fertility studies to date only compare point estimates of fertility at a particular time. He stressed the need for longitudinal data in order to discover the processes behind fertility among forced migrants. Although Keely questioned the feasibility of acquiring longitudinal data, Bradley Woodruff pointed out that some long-term camps do have fairly good birth registration systems. Allan Hill commented that a few pieces of data, such as a simple birth history, could be extremely useful and easy to obtain from medical assistance records or ration cards. Although many agreed that this information could be useful, some participants worried about data confidentiality.

Many conflicting factors both support and discourage the fertility of forced migrants, so it is likely to vary greatly depending on the specific situation. Black cautioned that in some situations women may either claim to be pregnant when they are not or hide a pregnancy, for a variety of reasons. Researchers and aid workers alike must be able to analyze the specifics of a given situation in order to understand how fertility will be affected. Better data, improved methods, and more research are needed in order to improve understanding of the phenomenon of fertility in forced migrant situations.

OPPORTUNITIES FOR FURTHER WORK

Potential Use of Sample Surveys

Courtland Robinson discussed how sample surveys, specifically, the Demographic and Health Surveys (DHS), could be used to measure and model successful reintegration of former refugees in their homelands. Because the upcoming survey for Cambodia already contains a question on migration, Robinson believes that adding just a few more questions about motivations for moving, places of residence, and timing of moves could help to identify refugees and internally displaced persons. Their demographic characteristics could then be compared with those of the rest of the population. Such analysis would help demographers to learn more about the relationships between forced migration, fertility, and mortality.

Robinson pointed out that following up with a migration survey in some of the original countries where DHS surveys were carried out could be very useful. Many of these countries are either refugee-producing or refugee-receiving or have experienced internal population displacement. A detailed follow-up survey might lead to new insights into the links between demographic processes for refugees and for internally displaced persons.

Many participants agreed that a small number of additional questions could produce a large amount of important data, but concerns were raised about increased costs and the burden to returnees. Burkholder pointed out that repatriated refugees might be underrepresented in surveys, so that samples might not be large enough to make comparisons. Sullivan questioned if DHS is the proper vehicle for conducting such surveys. Overall, however, there was general agreement that sample surveys of some type could be useful sources of information about refugees who have returned to their home countries.

Possibilities for Future Research and Collaboration

For the concluding session of the workshop, Myron Weiner and Allan Hill commented on the challenges that the research community faces in an era of ever-changing international norms regarding forced migration. Weiner noted the danger involved when forced migrant situations become highly politicized. For example, although the militarization of refugee camps is not a new phenomenon, it now poses a huge problem in the face of the principle of avoiding forced repatriation. In other words, the idea of not returning refugees to a perilous situation in their homeland takes on a much graver meaning if they are being attacked, coerced, or terrorized within the camps that are supposed to be safe havens. Meanwhile, global norms now advocate the eventual safe return of refugees to their country of origin, so fewer and fewer countries are willing to provide long-term asylum, despite the possible hazards of too hasty repatriation.

Weiner argued that in addition to improving data on forced migrants for relief purposes, researchers should focus on ways that data can be used for other policy purposes. Perhaps data could point to new solutions for preventing conflicts before they begin or for reconstructing communities after a conflict is over. As for specific research questions, he focused on several areas in which demographers could use existing data in order to discover more about the dynamics of the forced migration process. For example, demographers could try to discover the circumstances under which refugees are more likely to voluntarily be repatriated. Another possibility that Weiner raised is to study the causes of forced migration, especially when governments force people to move for security reasons, such as the Bangladesh movement of Bengalis into the Chittagong Hill tracts over the past 25 years. Finally, demographers could investigate the characteristics of populations in post-conflict societies.

All of these types of research can affect policy decisions significantly and can be done using approximate historical data, which, Black noted, are constantly collected by aid agencies but which are almost never analyzed later. He cautioned, however, that states might use the type of knowledge that could be gained from such research in order to further their own political agendas. For example, if demographers were to discover factors that could encourage repatriation, this information might be used to advocate early resettlement, even when it was not the right choice in a particular situation.

Allan Hill outlined several topics for which participants' comments suggested a need for future research and collaboration. First, there are structural issues related to the question of how and by whom further research within the field of forced migration will be coordinated. He emphasized the need for the right umbrella organization to oversee research activities. Keely speculated that existing networks would be useful, but not unless they include demographers and other social scientists in their discussions. Allan Hill also noted that funding and accountability to donors are important structural issues.

Allan Hill next highlighted some specific research issues. He argued that it is important to be able to classify different kinds of emergencies according to legal definitions and physical effects. This need for typologies of forced migration was recognized by many participants, but it may be one of the most difficult topics on which to agree. Allan Hill discussed the imperative to develop new measurement methods or to extend old methods for use in forced migration situations. Finally, research on health and morbidity assessment in populations under stress is needed. Waldman suggested that other areas of focus might include anthropometry, reproductive health needs, and sexual behavior in refugee camps.

Among practical issues, definitions were one that participants viewed as being in need of attention. If definitions could be standardized across sources, perhaps better estimates would result. This is unlikely to happen soon, though, and might only result in more consistent numbers, rather than more reliable ones.

As for other practical matters, Allan Hill and others suggested the possibility of implementing training workshops to teach field staff basic demographic techniques (such as sampling). Kenneth Hill urged that presentations be standardized for ease of comparison between sources. Participants also discussed the feasibility of creating field manuals that illustrate these techniques and contain model questionnaires. Many participants favored these ideas, but they emphasized the need to include nongovermental organizations and aid agencies in the process of developing them. Many manuals or guides may already exist and only need to be updated or revised.

Paul Spiegel advocated sharing information between nongovermental organizations and establishing standard reporting practices so that data are not just kept at the field level. Zlotnik pointed out that the new U.N. recommendations for migration statistics include guidelines for reporting statistics on refugees and asylum-seekers for the first time. Although contact persons are generally available in each country, it is often difficult to get information from them. Keely suggested that these persons could be brought together at a conference to discuss implementing the reporting guidelines and thus help to improve the state of the statistics.

Carolyn Makinson noted that, in her experience, nongovernmental organization field staff want training and are concerned about how to obtain a more accurate idea of the numbers, characteristics, and health status of the populations they are trying to help. Kimberly Hamilton expressed concern that practitioners do not know how to find baseline data for specific populations to use as reference points. Burkholder said that the Centers for Disease Control and Prevention are working with the World Health Organization in Geneva to develop a database of baseline figures for countries around the world.

Allan Hill also proposed that participants use the Internet in order to establish communication links between population scientists and humanitarian aid workers. Bennett suggested the use of existing newsgroups, such as the forced migration listserv at Oxford for this purpose. Other ideas offered by Allan Hill included a World Refugee Survey for the year 2000 and post-emergency assessments in order to evaluate the impact of aid on given situations for better future planning.

CONCLUSIONS

The workshop highlighted many ways in which demographers can assist in the study of forced migration. Social science techniques that are common to demography, such as sampling and surveys, can be very useful for estimating total populations, as well as fertility and mortality rates. Demographers can share data on baseline populations and their understanding of population dynamics with those who work in the field to give them a base of knowledge about the populations they serve. For the future, demographers should investigate the phenomenon of forced migration using existing historical data in order to better understand the process. In turn, nongovermental organizations and aid agencies should make the data that they collect in the field as accessible as possible to researchers so that it can be analyzed. Exchanges among population scientists and persons who work in the field of forced migration—at conferences, in training workshops, with manuals, or through the Internet—is bound to be productive. Consequently, lines of communication should be opened between demographers, humanitarian workers, and advocacy groups so that they can share their respective knowledge of population science, relief work, and public policy. Participants agreed that the Workshop on the Demography of Forced Migration was an important step toward more cooperation and knowledge sharing among these groups.

References

Argent, T.
  1997   Refugee Statistics: Myth, Reality, and Imperfect Guesses. Unpublished paper presented
          at the annual meeting of the Population Association of America, March 27-29, 1997.
          U.S. Committee for Refugees, Washington, D.C.
Bennett, J.
  1997   Forced Migration Within National Borders: The IDP Agenda. Unpublished paper pre-
          sented at the Workshop on the Demography of Forced Migration, Committee on Popula-
          tion, National Research Council, November 6-7, 1997. The Global IDP Survey, Oxford,
          England.
Bilsborrow, R.E., G. Hugo, A.S. Oberai, and H. Zlotnik
  1997   *International Migration Statistics: Guidelines for Improving Data Collection Systems.*
          Geneva, Switzerland: International Labor Organization.
Centers for Disease Control and Prevention
  1992   Famine-affected, refugee, and displaced populations: recommendations for public health
          issues. *Morbidity and Mortality Weekly Report* 41(No.RR-13):1-76.
Harrell-Bond, B., E. Voutira, and M. Leopold
  1992.   Counting the refugees: gifts, givers, patrons, and clients. *Journal of Refugee Studies* 5(3
          and 4).
Levine, D.B., K. Hill, and R. Warren, eds.
  1985   *Immigration Statistics: A Story of Neglect.* Panel on Immigration Statistics, Committee
          on National Statistics, National Research Council. Washington, D.C.: National Acad-
          emy Press.
Schmeidl, S.
  1995   From Root Cause Assessment to Preventive Diplomacy: Possibilities and Limitations of
          the Early Warning of Forced Migration. Unpublished doctoral dissertation, Department
          of Sociology, Ohio State University.

1997   Refugee Data and Sources: How Much Do They Differ and Why. Unpublished paper presented at The Workshop on the Demography of Forced Migration, Committee on Population, National Research Council, November 6-7, 1997. United Nations High Commissioner for Refugees, Geneva, Switzerland.

Toole, M.J. and R.J. Waldman
1997   The public health aspects of complex emergencies and refugee situations. *Annual Review of Public Health* 18:283-312.

Toole, M.J., P. Nieburg, and R.J. Waldman
1988   The association between inadequate rations, undernutrition prevalence, and mortality in refugee camps: case studies of refugee populations in eastern Thailand, 1979-1980, and eastern Sudan, 1984-1985. *Journal of Tropical Pediatrics* 34:218-224.

United Nations
1950   *Convention Relating to the Status of Refugees.* United Nations Conference of Plenipotentiaries on the Status of Refugees and Stateless Persons convened under General Assembly Resolution 429(V) of December 14, 1950. New York: United Nations.

1966   *Protocol Relating to the Status of Refugees.* United Nations General Assembly Resolution 2198(XXI) of December 16, 1966. New York: United Nations.

United Nations High Commissioner for Refugees
1994   Registration: A Practical Guide for Field Staff. Unpublished internal document. United Nations High Commissioner for Refugees, Geneva, Switzerland.

1997   *Refugees and Others of Concern to UNHCR: 1996 Statistical Overview.* Geneva, Switzerland: United Nations High Commissioner for Refugees.

United States Committee for Refugees
1997   *World Refugee Survey, 1997.* Washington: Immigration and Refugee Services of America.

Van Damme, W.
1995   Do refugees belong in camps? experiences from Goma and Guinea. *The Lancet* 346:360-362.

Wulf, D.
1994   *Refugee Women and Reproductive Health Care: Reassessing Priorities.* New York: Women's Commission for Refugee Women and Children.

Appendix

Workshop on the Demography of Forced Migration

Committee on Population
National Research Council of the National Academy of Sciences
2101 Constitution Avenue, NW
NAS Board Room
Washington, DC

November 6-7, 1997

AGENDA

November 6

POPULATION ESTIMATES

8:30   Continental breakfast

9:15   Welcome
        Faith Mitchell, National Research Council

9:30   What Do We Need to Know About the Descriptive Demography
        of Forced Migration?
        Charles Keely, Georgetown University

9:45   Comments
        Bela Hovy, U.N. High Commissioner for Refugees

10:00   Comments
        Thomas Argent, U.S. Committee for Refugees

10:15   Discussion

10:30   Break

10:45   Data Sources: How Much Do They Differ and Why?
           Susanne Schmeidl, Consultant,
           U.N. High Commissioner for Refugees

11:00   Comments
           Bela Hovy, UNHCR

11:15   Comments
           Thomas Argent, USCR

11:30   Comments
           Allan Hill, Harvard University

11:45   The Politics of Data Collection: Uses and Abuses
           Richard Black, University of Sussex

12:00   Discussion

12:15   Lunch

           POPULATION COMPOSITION AND VITAL RATES

1:15   How a DART (Disaster Assistance Response Team) Works
           Gregory Garbinsky, OFDA, USAID

1:45   The Experience in Estimating Population Composition and
           Mortality Rates
           Brent Burkholder, CDC

2:15   Comments
           Kenneth Hill, Johns Hopkins University

2:30   Comments
           Ronald Waldman, The BASICS Project

2:45   Break

3:00   Discussion

3:15   Thoughts on the Potential Use of Sample Surveys
           Courtland Robinson, Johns Hopkins University

3:30   Discussion

4:00   What Do We Know About Estimating Fertility Rates?
          Kenneth Hill, Johns Hopkins University

4:15   Discussion

5:00   Adjourn

6:00   Dinner — NAS Members' Room
          Guest speaker: The Honorable Thomas C. Sawyer
          "U.S. Refugee Policy: What Congress Needs to Know"

November 7

8:30   Continental Breakfast

9:15   Issues Relating to the Collection of Data on Internally Displaced
          Populations
          Jon Bennett, The Global IDP Survey

9:35   Comments
          Steven Hansch, Refugee Policy Group

9:50   Discussion

10:15   Summary: Populations, Composition and Vital Rates
          Charles Keely, Georgetown University

          RESEARCH AGENDA

10:30   Research Agenda for the Study of Forced Migration
          Myron Weiner, Massachusetts Institute of Technology

10:50   Comments
          Allan Hill, Harvard University

11:00   Break

11:15   Discussion: Possible themes for an NRC study

12:30   Lunch, Adjournment

SELECTED PUBLICATIONS
COMMITTEE ON POPULATION

Available from the National Academy Press (2101 Constitution Avenue NW, Washington, DC 20418; call 1-800-624-6242; many reports also available on line at: http://www.nap.edu):

Welfare, the Family, and Reproductive Behavior: Research Perspectives (1998)

The Immigration Debate: Studies on the Economic, Demographic, and Fiscal Effects of Immigration (1998)

From Death to Birth: Mortality Decline and Reproductive Change (1998)

Between Zeus and the Salmon: The Biodemography of Longevity (1997)

The New Americans: Economic, Demographic, and Fiscal Effects of Immigration (1997)

Premature Death in the New Independent States (1997)

Racial and Ethnic Differences in the Health of Older Americans (1997)

Reproductive Health in Developing Countries: Expanding Dimensions, Building Solutions (1997)

Changing Numbers, Changing Needs: American Indian Demography and Public Health (1996)

Fertility in the United States: New Patterns, New Theories (1996)[*]

Preventing and Mitigating AIDS in Sub-Saharan Africa: Research and Data Priorities for the Social and Behavioral Sciences (1996)

Demography of Aging (1994)

Population and Land Use in Developing Countries: Report of a Workshop (1993)

The Epidemiological Transition: Policy and Planning Implications for Developing Countries: Workshop Proceedings (1993)

Demographic Change in Sub-Saharan Africa (1993)

Demographic Effects of Economic Reversals in Sub-Saharan Africa (1993)

Social Dynamics of Adolescent Fertility in Sub-Saharan Africa (1993)

Factors Affecting Contraceptive Use in Sub-Saharan Africa (1993)

---

[*]A supplement to volume 22, *Population and Development Review*. Available from The Population Council, One Dag Hammarskjold Plaza, New York, NY 10017